VEGAN KETO COOKBOOK

Over 50 High-Fat Plant-Based Ketogenic Recipes to Heal Your Mind, Body and Soul

NICOLE JAMES

Text Copyright © Nicole James

All rights reserved. No part of this guide may be reproduced in any form without permission in writing from the publisher except in the case of brief quotations embodied in critical articles or reviews.

Legal & Disclaimer

The information contained in this book and its contents is not designed to replace or take the place of any form of medical or professional advice; and is not meant to replace the need for independent medical, financial, legal or other professional advice or services, as may be required. The content and information in this book has been provided for educational and entertainment purposes only.

The content and information contained in this book has been compiled from sources deemed reliable, and it is accurate to the best of the Author's knowledge, information and belief. However, the Author cannot guarantee its accuracy and validity and cannot be held liable for any errors and/or omissions. Further, changes are periodically made to this book as and when needed. Where appropriate and/or necessary, you must consult a professional (including but not limited to your doctor, attorney, financial advisor or such other professional advisor) before using any of the suggested remedies, techniques, or information in this book.

Upon using the contents and information contained in this book, you agree to hold harmless the Author from and against any damages, costs, and expenses, including any legal fees potentially resulting from the application of any of the information provided by this book. This disclaimer applies to any loss, damages or injury caused by the use and application, whether directly or indirectly, of any advice or information presented, whether for breach of contract, tort, negligence, personal injury, criminal intent, or under any other cause of action.

You agree to accept all risks of using the information presented inside this book.

You agree that by continuing to read this book, where appropriate and/or necessary, you shall consult a professional (including but not limited to your doctor, attorney, or financial advisor or such other advisor as needed) before using any of the suggested remedies, techniques, or information in this book.

TABLE OF CONTENTS

Introduction 8
   Download KETO SMOOTHIES eBook - completely FREE! 9
Chapter 1: The Vegan-Keto Diet 10
   What is the Vegan Diet? 11
   What are the Problems with this Diet? 13
   What is the Keto Diet? 25
   Challenges of the Keto Diet 27
   Can You Blend the Two? 28
   The Health Benefits of a Vegan-Keto Diet 30
Chapter 2: How to Follow the Vegan-Keto Diet 32
   What Can You Eat? 33
   What You Can't Eat? 36
   Vegan-Keto and Exercise 37
   Overcoming Keto Flu 38
   Dealing with Negative People 40
Chapter 3: A Vegan-Keto 7-day Meal Plan 41
   Meal Plan[13] 42
      Monday 42
      Tuesday 43
      Wednesday 44
      Thursday 45
      Friday 46
      Saturday 47
      Sunday 48
Chapter 4: Recipes 49
Plant-Based Main Meals 50
   Breakfast 51

- Flaxseed Waffles 52
- Polenta Frittata 53
- Hempheart Oatmeal 55
- Tofu Benedict 56
- Scrambled Tofu 58

Lunch or Dinner Entrees 59
- Eggplant Bird's Eye 60
- Portobello Burgers 61
- Vegan Sloppy Joes 62
- Jicama Sticks 63
- Stuffed Mushrooms with Spinach, Vegan Cheese, and Pine Nuts 64
- Stuffed Avocados with Vegan Cheese and Black Beans 65
- Spicy Lentil Soup 66
- Tofu or Soy Egg Salad on a Bed of Lettuce 68
- Black Bean Burgers 69
- Zucchini Lasagna 70
- Kelp Noodles with Avocado Pesto Sauce 72
- Creamy Roasted Red Pepper Soup 73
- Cream of Mushroom Soup 74
- Harissa Portobello Tacos 75

7 Sauces, Dressings, and Dips 77
- Spinach Artichoke Dip 78
- Jalapeno Hummus 79
- Spicy Peanut Sauce 80
- Vegan Ranch Dressing 81
- Vegan Italian Dressing 82
- Creamy Avocado Sauce 83
- Almond Feta 84

7 Vegan Fat Bombs 85
- Nutty Coconut Balls..86
- No Bake Oatmeal Fudge Bars 88
- Chocolate Almond Butter Cups......................................90
- Lemon Fat Bombs 91
- Pumpkin Pie Bites 92
- Green Truffles 93

7 Salads...94
- Palm Hearts Salad 95
- Rich Vegetable Salad 96
- Cajun Tempeh Chicken Salad 97
- Leafy Green Salad...98
- Southwestern Tofu Salad with Black Beans and Lime Dressing........99
- Vegan Chef's Salad 101
- Vegan Cobb Salad 102

7 Smoothies 103
- Iced Coffee 104
- Cinnamon Chocolate Breakfast Smoothie...................105
- Green Coffee Shake 106
- Coffee and Chocolate Smoothie 107
- Blueberry Smoothie 108
- Chocolate Almond Smoothie 109
- Lemon Ginger Green Smoothie 110

7 Desserts...111
- Chia Pudding 112
- Coconut Chocolate Cups...113
- Poached Pears with Dark Chocolate 114
- Blueberry Soy Cheesecake..115

- No-Crust Apple Pie...116
- Walnuts with Dark Chocolate...117
- Chocolate Silk Pie with Almond Crust..118
- Download KETO SMOOTHIES eBook - completely FREE!...................119
- References..120

Introduction

Can the vegan-keto diet even be done? At first glance, these two diets are polar opposites. Vegan diets call for high carbs and low fat from plant sources, while the ketogenic diet calls for high fat and low carbs from animal sources. Yet somehow, the two can be blended together into a magical diet that guarantees fat loss, lower cholesterol, better energy, and superior brain health.

No matter why you want to be vegan, eating vegan does not limit you from the high-fat diet, also known as the ketogenic diet. This book will teach you all that you need to know about creating this diet to nourish your body and support your metabolism. It will also teach you various tips for incorporating exercise, getting adequate nutrients, dealing with negative influences, and avoiding the keto flu.

At the end, there are various recipes that can help you make your diet far from bland so that you are inclined to stick to it. There is also a series of tips on how to cook vegan-keto. Our seven-day meal plan will help you adjust to this diet and follow through.

By the end of this book, you will be an expert on the vegan-keto diet. You will be ready to start this amazing diet and glean the many health benefits that come with it.

Download KETO SMOOTHIES eBook - completely FREE!

Low carb smoothies are among the best treats on the ketogenic diet. So good and nutritious, they make meals simple and quick, and can also be effective instant cures when you're fighting the dreaded keto flu.

They're perfect anytime, but especially when you're not hungry but you need to fill up. The best keto smoothie recipes are those engineered to help you achieve your fat, protein and micronutrient macros while staying very low carb.

Go to NJKETO.COM/SMOOTHIES and get instant free access.

Limited time offer.

Chapter 1: The Vegan-Keto Diet

Welcome to the vegan keto diet! The vegan keto diet is a solution for those who want to lose weight and attain better health with the ketogenic diet…without all of the animal fats and proteins typical of the diet. Let's review how both veganism and ketogenic diet work so that you can understand how to meld these two diets together into one powerfully healthy and slimming combo.

What is the Vegan Diet?

A good vegan diet ideally contains no animal products of any kind. Vegans typically follow this diet because they care about animals and the environment and have concerns with the violations to both performed daily by the meat industry. However, the vegan diet is not just conscientious. It also have vast benefits in improving blood glucose control.[1] Most vegan consumers also report dramatic weight loss results.[1] Studies have found that vegans tend to have lower BMIs than non-vegans.[1]

The vegan diet is not always as straightforward as just avoiding animal products. In fact, finding how to avoid animal products while still gaining proper nourishment requires a decent amount of math. There are a few variations of veganism:

- **The whole-food vegan diet:** This diet is restricted to only whole foods that are not processed in any way, such as fruits, vegetables, whole grains, legumes, nuts, and seeds.
- **The raw-food vegan diet:** This diet calls for whole foods cooked below 118°F (48°C) or not cooked at all.
- **80/10/10:** This diet calls for raw food without fat-rich plants such as nuts or avocados. Consumers are suppoed to munch on raw fruits and greens instead. This diet options is also known as the low-fat, raw-food vegan diet or the fruitarian diet.
- **The Starch Solution:** This one is the different from the low-fat, raw food vegan diet because it calls for high carbs from sources like potatoes or rice, rather than fruit. Otherwise, these two variances are very similar.
- **Raw till 4:** This is where one eats raw foods until 4, and then cooked plants after 4.
- **The junk-food vegan diet:** Some people are vegan but rely on heavily processed "junk" foods that are vegan, such as cheese or snacks.

The vegan-keto diet is unlike other vegan diets because it focuses more on getting high fat and high protein, rather than high carbs. In fact, you should not be eating many carbs on this diet at all. Contrary to what it may seem, there is no need to consume junk food, even of the vegan variety, just to gain these nutrients. You can gain plenty of fat and protein from whole, raw foods like avocados, nuts, and coconuts, and supplements such as Spirulina, wheat grass juice powder, coconut oils, and vegetable oils.

What are the Problems with this Diet?

No diet is perfect, and the vegan diet has some of its own limitations. The main concern with veganism is the potential for nutrient deficiencies inherent to eating only plant-based foods.

One huge challenge with this diet is that many foods have animal products in them, even if you don't realize it. A "vegetarian" soup may still contain some things like butter, cheese, or even chicken stock. You may find little bits of animal products in almost everything you order at a restaurant. Cross contamination is common, where an animal product touches one of the ingredients in your vegan meal. Even salads are not safe, with animal fats in the dressing or butter in the croutons.

Many vegans become overwhelmed finding true vegan options. They may either give up on the diet, or else stop taking in the proper nutrients as they avoid too many foods. Malnutrition is still possible, even if you are eating adequate helpings of food each day, because you are not gaining the nutrients essential for survival. The effects of malnutrition go beyond losing weight and also cause things like fatigue, depression, anxiety, and anemia.

Adequate daily nutrition is a challenge on this diet. But taking in enough nutrients each day is more than possible. You just have to seek proper foods that contain the necessary nutrients. There are a vast variety of vegan food options that will nourish your body properly.

The daily nutrient requirements for the average person is as follows[2]:

- 64 grams of protein per day
- 30 grams of fiber per day
- 58 grams of fat per day

- Vitamin A   900 µg per day
- Thiamin   1.2 mg per day
- Riboflavin   1.3 mg per day
- Niacin   16 mg per day
- Vitamin B6   1.3 mg/day*
- Vitamin B12   2.4 µg per day
- Folate   400 µg per day
- Vitamin C   45 mg per day
- Calcium   1000 mg per day
- Iodine   150 µg per day
- Iron   8 mg per day
- Magnesium   400 mg per day
- Potassium   3800 mg per day
- Sodium   460-920 mg per day
- Zinc   14 mg per day

It is recommended that you eat more colorful foods on this diet.[3] Don't just limit yourself to greens. Having a rainbow of colorful bell peppers, cauliflower, and other such foods is a good idea to make sure you gain more nutrients. Focusing on super foods is also a good idea because these foods contain a plethora of nutrients, often your entire daily requirement, or RDA.

Some super foods include[4]:

- **Acai** – Acai is a berry that is rich in antioxidants, amino acids, essential fatty acids, fiber, phytosterols, and trace minerals. It is known for its weight loss properties. Plus you can use as a flavoring.

- **Aloe Vera** – high in antioxidants, amino acids, aenzymes, calcium, magnesium, and potassium.

- **Avocado** – Avocados are a great source of fat. They actually lower cholesterol and improve heart health. They also contain omega fatty acids, potassium, folic acid, vitamin E, lutein, and other vitamins and minerals.

- **Beans and Lentils**- These are staples for vegans because of their high fat and protein content. They can provide calcium and fiber as well.

- **Beet Leaves**- Eating these leaves in a salad can give you a plethora of fiber, folate, magnesium, calcium, and antioxidants.

- **Blueberries** – Blueberries are the number one source of antioxidants. They have high fiber and are naturally hydrating. In addition, they are a sweet treat without high sugar or high calories.

- **Broccoli** – These dark greens boast fiber, antioxidants, vitamin C, calcium, and iron. It is the best natural source of iron since the vitamin C works with iron to make it more easily absorbed without upsetting your tummy like iron supplements tend to do. Some evidence suggests that it helps with avoiding diabetes and cancer.

- **Buckwheat** – This is a great source of carbs without adding too many calories. They are extremely high in fiber and amino acids for cellular health. You can effectively lower cholesterol with buckwheat.

- **Cabbage** – Eating fermented or fresh or steamed cabbage will give you a nice influx of fiber, vitamin C, and iodine. Plus, cabbage has sulfur compounds to boost your immunity.

- **Carrots** – The vitamin K in carrots is good for your eyes. They also have vitamin A to help with eye health and detoxifying the body. They also boast large amounts of vitamin K, B vitamins, potassium, phosphorus, magnesium, and folate.

- **Cinnamon** – Cinnamon is an excellent spice to use, not only for its flavor, but for its extremely potent antioxidant properties. It has shown promise in research trials for lowering the blood sugar in diabetics.
- **Citrus** – Get all of the vitamin C you need for immune system function with citru fruits. Also gain a healthy dose of fiber and potassium, which aids with pain relief and muscle relaxation.
- **Coconut** – Coconut will be a common theme in this book for its excellent healthy fats and triglycerides. The fat in coconut is easy to burn, making it ideal for both vegan and ketogenic dieters. It can also lower cholesterol and help you lose weight. Use it in food or use coconut oil for cooking. The health benefits of coconut oil go beyond diet, and can be used as treatment for skin conditions or as a natural laxative.
- **Dark Chocolate** – Don't eat the processed chocolate that is high in sugar. Stick with dark chocolate, which is

unsweetened and rather bitter in taste. This dark chocolate is one of Nature's richest sources of antioxidants, without being high on the glycemic index. Plus, it does not cause blood sugar spikes.

- **Figs** – Figs are excellent sources of antioxidants and fiber. Plus, they boast vitamin A and most forms of vitamin B. They can be sources of calcium and iron. They have pectin which is associated with lower cholesterol and lower blood pressure. They have phosphorus as well.

- **Flax and Chia Seeds** – You can get a big amount of fiber and amino acids in just a few teaspoons of these seeds, mixed into food or ground up and used as a flour substitute. Flax seeds contain lots of lignans, which are potent antioxidants that may have anticancer properties. Chia seeds are high in omega fatty acids, calcium, potassium, and iron.

- **Garlic, Leeks, and Onions** – These vegetables are of the Allium family and share many of the same properties. They are particularly good for fighting disease with their high levels of sulfur compounds. Their antioxidants can help fight aging.

- **Ginger** – Ginger is a warming herb that you can make excellent teas from, and you can use it to add flavor to your meals. It can calm your stomach if you are sick. The anti-inflammatory chemicals called gingerols work to fight pain and boost your immunity.

- **Green Tea** – Green tea has been cited by many studies as a source of antioxidants to help heal wounds, boost heart health, and even assist with the treatment of cancer.

- **Maca** – Maca root is actually great for enhancing your energy levels and your fertility. It has complex carbs, also called good carbs, and fiber and protein. It has many vitamins, including vitamin C, and zinc, iron, and copper.

- **Miso** - Miso is an Asian seasoning made from fermented rice, barley, or soybeans. It is a great source of sodium and protein. Plus it offers manganese, vitamin K, and fiber.

- **Mushrooms** – These are one of the best sources of vegan protein and can even replace meat in things like burgers.

They are one of the only food-based sources of vitamin D. They have high amounts of fiber. Plus they have potassium, B vitamins, and selenium. There are many different options to choose from to glean health benefits without calories.

- **Oregano** – Oregano contains many vitamins and antioxidants. But it is also a great source of omega fatty acids. On top of that, it has unique antibacterial properties. Use it as a spice on any dish to get a dose of calcium.

- **Peas** - Peas are rather unassuming but they are a rich source of protein without adding many calories to your diet. They also have trace metals like magnesium, copper, zinc, and iron. They have lots of vitamin K, manganese, vitamin C, fiber, B vitamins, phosphorus, vitamin A, and potassium. These are excellent vegan sources of protein to replace meat along with beans. They are recommended for those with diabetes or heart issues.

- **Peppers** – The more colorful foods are the best for nutrition, as you will find with peppers. They have lots of carotenoids to help with your eyes. They also have lots of vitamins A, B, C, and K. They contain lots of lycopene and lutein. Hotter peppers have capsaicin which is an antioxidant and has been indicated to help with weight loss, sinus issues, and inflammation.

- **Pumpkin** – This orange squash is rich in carotenoids, which help with skin, vision, and hair and nail growth. It is a rich source of fiber, vitamin E, vitamin C, magnesium, and potassium. Munching on the seeds will give you protein and zinc.

- **Seaweed** – This is a true superfood. It is best known for its high iodine content, which serves your thyroid. But it also contains potassium, iron, calcium, and magnesium. It contains the vitamins A and C. You can use it as a salt substitute to lower sodium if you are eating low-sodium.

- **Sesame Seed** – These little seeds have something called lignans, a special type of fiber that is shown to reduce cholesterol and blood pressure. They also have loads of vitamin E for skin health. You can gain trace metals and protein from these seeds as well. It can boost your fat intake.

- **Spinach** – Spinach is a super food because just one cup has more than your daily required intake of vitamin A, vitamin K, manganese, folate, calcium, fiber, magnesium, and protein. It also has carotenoids, which can fight cancer. **Sprouts** – The sprouts of any grain, including alfalfa, contain enzymes that can aid in digestion. They are high in fiber. They contain many antioxidants.
- **Tomatoes** – Tomatoes are great sources of vitamin, vitamin K, and vitamin A. They are also great for keeping blood platelets from sticking together. Some studies have linked them to preventing cancers. Their lycopene content is great for cellular health and reversing aging.
- **Turmeric** – This spice is what gives curry its flavor. It is best known for its antibacterial and antiseptic abilities. It's been indicated in the elimination of many cancers and can relieve pain by acting as a natural anti –inflammatory. Some studies have indicated that it helps with the liver. Finally, it is great for reversing aging and lowering cholesterol because of its curcumin and antioxidant properties.

- **Walnuts** – You will notice we often refer to walnuts in the recipes below because they are so good for you. They are an excellent source of omega fatty acids, copper, and manganese, all metals the body needs in low doses. They also have antioxidants to reverse aging on the body and help with heart health. Finally, they offer magnesium and calcium for bone health.
- **Wheat and Barley Grass** – While you cannot eat grains in high amounts on this diet, you can enjoy the benefits of the grasses that grow these grains. Oat, wheat, and barley grass are all green cereal juices. They are notably high in chlorophyll, which mimics hemoglobin in humans and creates a more oxygen-rich environment in the body. They are incredibly rich sources of vitamin A, carotenoids, vitamin E, and B vitamins. They have minerals like essential amino acids, iron, calcium, potassium, phosphorus, magnesium, and zinc. Their properties can help balance hormones and cleanse the body, while also deodorizing you and getting rid of the body odor that often accompanies the keto diet.

Beyond eating super foods, you should also be sure to eat things like calcium-rich cheese or other food options that are enriched with calcium.[3] A daily multivitamin is also recommended.[3] But generally, you can get most of your daily needs from food alone. In addition, you will find that sunlight is an excellent source of vitamin D. Many vegan foods have added vitamins and minerals to help vegans meet their daily needs, so you may be able to get your nutrient requirements met entirely through diet and sun exposure.

What is the Keto Diet?

The ketogenic diet, hereafter called the "keto diet," is a diet that forces your body into intense fat-burning mode. You must avoid all sugars and carbohydrates and nourish your body with only protein and fat. Doing this will cause your body to enter ketosis, a state where your body burns fat for energy since it has no sugar available to burn instead. Weight loss on this diet can be intense and incredible.

While we go into more detail on how to execute this diet properly in the next chapter, here is a brief overview over how this diet actually works:

Normally you eat carbs. In fact, most diets call for more carbs than any other nutrient. Thus, your body converts that to glucose, which feeds your cells. But the keto diet has almost no carbs. This forces your liver to start converting the fats it gets into ketones and fatty acids. Now your body must use ketone bodies to run, rather than glucose. Only 5% of your cells cannot use these as a source of fuel, which is why you are supposed to consume 5% of your diet in carbs even on the keto diet.[12] Ketones becomes your body's main energy source on this diet. This means that your body will burn all of its fat stores, causing you to lose weight in a process called ketosis, but it will also use the fat in your diet to get energy.

The only way to reach this state of ketosis is to almost completely eliminate carbs from your diet. Some carbs are allowable, such as a few berries in the morning, as long as the carbs and sugar is negligible. The recommended daily carb intake is around 10-35 grams, which is an apple or a glass of milk[5]. Bear in mind that there are good carbs, which come from whole foods, and bad carbs, which come from processed sources, wheat, or white grains like white rice. Generally, you need to consume 80-90% of your daily calories in fat.[5]

Most people get all of this fat from animal products, like bacon, hot dogs, and milk. Some people allow for more fruits and vegetables, but this is not necessarily what the diet allows. Following a true keto diet sticks within the confines of the carb deficit very strictly, which means fruits and veggies are not allowed in high amounts.

The diet works by making your body burn fat. But a recent study has found that the weight loss is truly due to the fact that you are restricting carbs.[5] By not eating carbs, you reduce your cravings for them and stop wanting them eventually. This means that the diet gets easier to follow the longer you go with it.

To see if you are in ketosis, you can use Ketostix or some other ketone-measuring device to see if there are adequate ketones in your urine. If you are not at a high enough level of ketones, your body is not in ketosis.

The keto diet thus appears to exclude vegetarians and vegans, since it calls for so much use of animal fats and proteins. Butter, cheese, and meat are the cornerstones of the keto diet. But the reality is that you can follow the keto diet and still be vegan, especially in this day and age with many revolutions in health food.

Challenges of the Keto Diet

The keto diet has two primary challenges that followers face.

The first is the initial unpleasant symptoms that occur as your body cleanses itself of carbs. This cleanse can be rigorous and uncomfortable and is often referred to as "the keto flu." People enter this diet not expecting to suddenly feel nauseated, crampy, exhausted, and downright sick. But the keto flu is temporary and will pass. Some other issues with this diet include smelly breath. This can be helped with gum and proper oral hygiene, as well as eating some fruit.

The other challenge is carb cravings themselves. People on this diet will eliminate carb cravings, but it takes time. Carbs and sugar are actually very addictive. Your body comes to rely on them for fulfillment. Without them, the body goes into shock and starts to crave them like nothing else. The cravings can be fierce, but you can fight through them. Eventually they go away on their own and you no longer want carbs as your body adjusts to the new diet. Overcoming the cravings initially can be hard, however.

Can You Blend the Two?

Can you blend the vegan and keto diets? The short answer is, absolutely! The vegan keto diet will get you into amazing shape and help detox your body so that you feel your best. The long answer is that these two diets can be blended and you can put your body into ketosis without eating any animal products, but you have to take care to gain enough protein from plant sources. While this can pose a challenge, it is certainly possible, and you will learn how in this book.

The most important thing is to gain protein from plant sources. While fat does play a role in forcing your body into full ketosis, it is only a small part of the picture. Science has shown that protein is actually far more nourishing and fulfilling than fat. Getting protein is thus much more important than getting fat. Since plants are seldom good sources of fat, this bodes well for you if you are starting this diet.

However, some plants are still great sources of fat. One such source would be avocados, which contain lots of monounsaturated fat. There are also plant oils that offer fat. You can still gain fat from eating a vegan diet. MUFAs are actually extremely great sources of nourishment linked to losing abdominal fat.

It may seem weird that eating a type of fat can make you lose fat. But MUFAs work quite a bit differently than other types of fat, such as saturated fats. Without going into complex chemistry, this is because MUFAs give you good cholesterol which helps your blood vessels retain their shape, without adding bad cholesterol.[6] They reduce the risk of heart disease and help cut abdominal fat[6]. They basically keep things moving in your body and provide you with dense, energy-rich calories that are perfect for the vegan-keto diet. To get your high fat intake for the keto diet, you can rely on foods high in MUFAs, but you should also eat foods that are high in protein to give you more energy.

Another thing to note is that diet alone is not the only key to a healthy lifestyle. To truly be at your best shape, you need to exercise. Getting at least thirty minutes of exercise three times a week (preferably more) is a good guideline for keeping in shape. Many people believe that exercise will help you lose weight, but this is a diet myth. Exercise will help trim you down if you also lose fat through your diet by making your muscles show. You can gain a sleek or even muscular body through exercise, but your routine must be paired with diet. Eating an unhealthy diet that keeps fat on your body while exercising will not allow you to shed pounds in most cases. However, the keto diet and vegan diets, especially when blended together, are excellent for bringing about fat loss, meaning that they will help you gain an excellent physique when paired with exercise.

Getting adequate fluids is also essential. If you are on this diet, be sure to be getting at least 6-8 glasses of water a day. Adding powdered vegan electrolytes to your water is also a good idea, provided that the supplement you choose does not contain any sugar. Avoid things like Gatorade, as these drinks have high sugar content and can throw your body out of ketosis.

The Health Benefits of a Vegan-Keto Diet

We already covered how you can gain a great physique with this diet. But it also has many other great things in store for your body and mind. This diet, when performed right, is extremely healthy. It will not cause you to become malnourished. You can glean excellent nutrition and countless health benefits from this diet.

- Originally keto was developed to help reduce seizures in children.[5] To this day, nutritionists can't explain why it works, but for some reason it does. This means that if you have epilepsy, you can reduce seizures with this diet.
- The keto diet is also associated with fewer neurodegenerative diseases, such as Alzheimer's, Parkinson's, and migraines.[7]
- You can reduce your risk of heart disease by essentially eliminating body fat, cholesterol and other issues with this diet.[6]
- You can achieve a healthy weight.[6]
- You have more energy naturally.[7] You can find more energy to do the things you love and exercise without being bogged down by carbs.
- This means you will also increase your athletic endurance because lactic acid will no longer be such an issue.[7]
- Reduce the risk of developing diabetes by curbing sugar.[7]
- Reduce the risk of metabolic syndrome, a group of symptoms containing things like high blood pressure, high cholesterol, and high blood sugar which can lead to stroke, diabetes, heart disease, obesity, blood clots, and even cancer.
- The World Health Organization has classified meats as a Level 1 carcinogen, meaning it can cause cancer. So eating this diet can lower your risk of developing cancer.[7]
- It can effectively remove skin issues like acne, psoriasis, and rashes caused by wheat intolerance.[8]
- It can be easier on your digestion because the human digestive system is not meant to consume lots of heavy meats or processed foods that are high in carbs.[8]

- Fats and proteins suppress ghrelin, the hormone that makes you feel hungry. This means that you will feel fuller and have fewer food cravings on this diet. Your tendency to overeat will diminish.[8]
- Blending the keto and vegan diets eliminates some of the issues that people exclusively following either diet face. Vegans face the issue of not getting enough nutrients, while keto users tend to face the issue of too many fats from unhealthy sources.

So there you have it. The vegan keto diet! Now read on to learn how to safely do this diet so that you gain the ultimate in nutrition and other health benefits.

Chapter 2: How to Follow the Vegan-Keto Diet

The vegan keto diet is a new trend in the diet world. But there are guidelines that keep you from going it alone. You can make this diet safe, healthy, and powerful by following the guidelines to ensure you get adequate daily nutrition.

What Can You Eat?

You can eat anything that is low carb and plant-based. That actually gives you many options!

You may be wondering just how to balance all of this information into one comprehensive diet. Here is a rough guideline of what you must get in your diet:

- 75% of your calories should come from fat.
- 20% from protein
- 5% from carbs

Keep your carb intake under 50 grams to stay in ketosis. Regularly test your urine, at least once a day, with Ketostix from your local pharmacy to ensure you are still in ketosis. If you are not, consider lowering your carb intake.

The main key to this diet is to include many plant-based meals. Choose vegetables that have low carbs and high fat or protein content.[8] There are many plants that boast excellent sources of protein.

You want to focus on low-carb vegetables. These include things like leafy greens, asparagus, carrots, onions, cauliflower, onions, mushrooms, eggplant, artichokes, kale, peppers, turnips, tomatoes, celery, Brussel sprouts, and cucumbers.[8] Do you notice that many of these foods are also super foods listed in the first chapter? You can make delicious salads, soups, or consume these steamed or raw. Keep in mind that steaming or consuming veggies raw will give you the highest nutritional yield.

Believe it or not, you can eat some fruits on this diet as well. Consider these fruits that have low carbs: blackberries, blueberries, strawberries, raspberries, cherries, citrus fruits, apples, apricots, and plums. These fruits should be eaten in moderation, but they offer enough carbs to meet your daily limit as well as vitamin C, antioxidants, and other such nutritional properties.

You should also try to find low-carb vegan food options, such as cheeses, milks, and vegan meat alternatives. There are actually vegan bacons, vegan burgers, and vegan hot dogs. A trip to the health food store can help you find everything you need.[8] These foods have lots of fat and protein to help sustain you and make your diet both vegan and ketogenic.

When you cook, use lots of coconut oil. Olive and other plant oils are also fine, but coconut oil generally has the best and highest fat content. Adding a few slices of avocado to every meal can also up the healthy fat content. Most of what you eat will be vegetables, so consider adding healthy plant oils to your salads and when you cook to gain more nutrition in one fell swoop. Palm oil, peanut oil, soybean oil, coconut oil, olive oil, and corn oil are all excellent sources of fat. Adding a handful or chia or flaxseeds to the top of your salad can further add to the protein and fiber you need.

For starters, try to get in a nutritious health shake to kick start your day. Shakes and smoothies are great ways to add lots of nutrition in one simple drink. They are easy to make, as well – just blend the ingredients with a few ice cubes and some coconut or almond milk for a delicious blend.

For snacks, munch on some walnuts or seaweed. Carrots also make a great super food snack option. Some of the time, you may crave something a bit more substantial, something that emulates carbs. This is when you can utilize chia seeds, hemp hearts, or flax seeds to make high-fiber, low-carb treats like waffles, pita bread, and sandwich wraps.

Getting protein from plants can be a challenge. This is why you should consume lots of **tempeh**, natto, nutritional yeast, spirulina, nuts and seeds, vegan tofu, wheatgrass juice (which doesn't have the carbs of wheat or wheat germ), and seaweed. Also consider lots of nuts, and peanut butter that has no carbs.[9]

You should also consider eating more fermented foods, like pickles and kimchi. These foods will give you the sodium and protein you need.

Now you may fear that you will start to get bored from eating the same things every day. This is where seasonings come into play. You can season a bowl of green beans different ways and get a new dish every time. You can cut open an avocado and add seasonings and vegan cheese to make a snack one day, and then the next eat seaweed sprinkled with sea salt for a snack. You can really experiment and create new things without following the same rote, day in, day out. This book contains many recipes that will make this diet interesting, and you can find even more online. Spicing up this diet is essential. Just ensure that your seasoning have no added carbs or non-vegan ingredients. Usually health food stores or online stores stock seasonings that don't have any animal ingredients.

What You Can't Eat?

Generally, focusing on what you can eat is more encouraging than focusing on what you can't. Seeing a long list of no-no foods can be very discouraging and can make you feel defeated. But it is useful to know some of the foods that may pose risks in slipping you out of ketosis. We will try to keep this as short and painless as possible.

Say no to:

- Anything with wheat, rice, corn, or other grains, including pastas, breads, and wraps
- Tropical fruits
- Dried fruits
- Animal-based foods like cheese, yogurt, ghee, butter, cream, eggs, meat, and meat products
- Beans and legumes of all kinds
- Bananas
- Fruit smoothies
- Fruit juices
- Fruit syrups
- Yams
- Parsnips
- Corn
- Yucca
- Cherry Tomatoes
- All sugars and sweeteners (some honey is OK in moderation)[10]

Vegan-Keto and Exercise

You may wonder how to blend this diet and exercise. If you work out, you have likely been told that you need carbs to fuel your workout. But in fact, working out on the vegan keto diet can increase your energy and endurance without making you slack on your workouts. So you can safely exercise while eating this way. Exercise is actually recommended for a healthy lifestyle.

So how do you gain the extra energy for exercise? Will you get too fatigued on the vegan keto diet? The truth is that you don't require carbs to fuel workouts.[10] You simply need more calories. This means that you can increase your fat intake and get more calories to accommodate a more active lifestyle. Carbs are just not needed.

How much should you increase your fat intake? Generally, for a moderately active person, men should eat between 2,000 and 2,500 calories per day and women should eat between 1,800 and 2,000.[11] But heavy exercise requires more to be added to that baseline. The best option is to visit an online calorie calculator because the calories you burn doing different types of exercise varies widely. That calculator can help you see how much you burn so that you can add that amount to your caloric intake. Livestrong has an excellent one that you can use, or you can find a keto diet app for your smart phone that lets you enter your activity levels and food to calculate your daily calorie needs and see if your meals fall into your prescribed range.

It is also true that you may need to take a break or at least slow down on exercise when you first start this diet. Many people report feeling fatigued on this diet at first. But this will pass and then you can freely exercise as you see fit.

Overcoming Keto Flu

If you are new to the keto diet, you will probably encounter the keto flu during the first few days. This flu affects most people who start this diet, so you are not alone. Keto flu can pose a hurdle that makes many people give up. Keep in mind that even as you feel awful, you will feel better soon if you just stick with the diet. Giving up on the diet will cause you to revert back to your carb-dependent state, and then you will endure the keto flu all over again if you ever choose to follow this diet again.

How to know when you have keto flu:[12]

- Exhaustion
- Sugar cravings
- Headaches and muscle aches
- Loss of appetite
- Dehydration
- Bad breath
- Nausea
- Constipation
- Diarrhea
- Heartburn
- Low sex drive
- Low energy for working out
- Moodiness
- Insomnia
- Vomiting
- High cholesterol
- Kidney stones

No one knows exactly what triggers the keto flu. The most likely explanation is that your body is busy kicking out carbs and cleansing itself, which can make you feel very sick. Another explanation is that you are actually withdrawing from sugar. Yet another explanation is electrolyte imbalance from improper fluid intake to accommodate the metabolic changes your body is naturally going through. [12]

The first key is to avoid getting dehydrated. Drinking enough water is very important on the keto diet. This diet makes it easy to lose electrolytes unless you keep hydrated and use electrolyte supplements.[12]

Another key is to consume enough sodium for electrolyte balancing, as well. Adding some sea salt to your veggies and buying vegan products with high sodium content is a good idea. Plus, salt adds flavor. [12]

Also, ensure you are getting enough calories by carefully reading food labels or looking up the veggies you eat in a calorie counter. A keto calorie counter app can be a useful tool at this point. Not getting enough calories can cause brain fog, depression, anemia, and exhaustion. You can minimize these symptoms by eating enough.[12]

Taking a week to rest is also helpful as you start out. Remember that keto flu resolves on its own after a week or so. You won't feel this way forever. Take it easy for a week as your body withdraws from sugar and adjusts its metabolism to burning ketone bodies.[12]

Dealing with Negative People

As you may already know if you tried eating vegan or any other diet, you will be met with resistance and even hostility from others when you attempt to change your diet. Your family may complain about your diet choices, or may try to tempt you with foods that will violate your dietary restrictions. You know, the grandmother who insists that you need meat to stay healthy or the husband/wife who brings home fast food and fresh bread from the bakery. Kids can especially make this diet hard, as they refuse to follow the diet because they hate veggies and insist on eating junk food.

The best thing for you to do is stand your ground. Just because other people don't like your diet does not mean that you need to give up on it. Tell people to please respect your diet and politely but firmly refuse their offerings of food. Tell very persistent people that your diet is not up for debate and you do not wish to discuss the matter any further. Remove yourself from situations where people seem to be dead-set on getting you to abandon your diet.

When negative people start to get you down, it can be helpful to turn to supportive communities. You can find vegan-keto forums and groups online, where you can meet like-minded people and share support and tips. You can also find their encouragement uplifting and motivational so that you stick with the diet.

Before going to parties, be sure to pack your own food or send a note ahead to the host. That way, you will have something to eat, even if the food at the party does not meet your specifications.

You cannot expect others to follow your diet, but you can expect them to respect it.

Chapter 3: A Vegan-Keto 7-day Meal Plan

To kick start your new diet, it is helpful to follow a strict seven-day meal plan for the first week. This gets your body used to going vegan-keto and also helps you develop the new lifestyle habits necessary for this diet. Once you have established your new eating patterns, you can begin to come up with your own recipes and form your own meal plan using different recipes. One of the best tips to keep on this diet is to make it interesting, and to add lots of new recipes to your repertoire. Keeping it delicious and interesting will keep you invested in the diet.

Meal Plan[13]

Monday

- **Breakfast**: High-Fiber Cereal with Berries
- **Lunch**: Spicy lentil soup, plus a salad of leafy greens with avocado
- **Snack**: Seaweed and peanuts
- **Dinner**: Grilled eggplant bird's eye, a vegetable salad with crumbly almond feta on top
- **Dessert**: Chocolate Coconut Cups

Tuesday

- **Breakfast**: Hempheart oatmeal with fruit
- **Lunch**: Spicy Tempeh with a leafy green vegetable salad and avocado cream dressing
- **Snack**: Celery stuffed with vegan peanut butter or hummus
- **Dinner**: Portobello burgers stuffed with vegan white cheese and steamed Brussel sprouts with cinnamon and vegan butter
- **Dessert**: Chia pudding with blueberries

Wednesday

- **Breakfast**: Flaxseed waffles
- **Lunch**: A leafy vegetable salad with cooked or raw Tofu chunks
- **Snack**: Steamed kale with vegan cheese and steamed tomatoes, mushrooms, and pine nuts
- **Dinner**: Kelp noodles with Avocado Pesto sauce
- **Dessert**: Poached Pears with dark chocolate melted on top

Thursday

- **Breakfast**: Polenta frittata
- **Lunch**: Spiced lentil soup, a salad with sliced avocados
- **Snack**: Jicama Sticks with Jalapeno Hummus
- **Dinner**: Salad with tofu
- **Dessert**: No-Crust apple pie

Friday

- **Breakfast**: Scrambled Tofu
- **Lunch**: Cajun Tempeh Chicken Salad, collard greens steamed with corn oil
- **Snack**: Spinach and Artichoke Dip, raw no-carb veggies for dipping
- **Dinner**: Vegan Sloppy Joes, leafy green salad
- **Dessert**: Blueberry soy cheesecake (crustless)

Saturday

- **Breakfast**: Green smoothie
- **Lunch**: Palm heart Salad, steamed cabbage with vegan bacon bits
- **Snack**: Mushrooms stuffed with spinach, vegan cheese, and pine nuts
- **Dinner**: Avocados stuffed with vegan cheese and black beans
- **Dessert**: walnuts covered in melted dark chocolate

Sunday

- **Breakfast**: A coffee smoothie
- **Lunch**: Soy egg salad on a bed of lettuce
- **Snack**: cucumber slices with spicy peanut sauce
- **Dinner**: Black bean burgers with vegan cheese and a salad
- **Dessert**: Chocolate Silk Pie with almond crust

Chapter 4: Recipes

Here are some recipes to get you started. Most of them fit into the seven-day meal plan, while there are some extras as well.

When you finish your seven-day plan, you will need to replenish your arsenal of great recipes. Otherwise, you run the risk of appetite fatigue, a state where you are so sick of eating the same thing that it actually makes you sick to eat. When you hit appetite fatigue, you run the risk of abandoning your diet. So follow some more unique recipes to prevent this from happening.

Plant-Based Main Meals

Breakfast

Flaxseed Waffles

Ingredients

- 2 cups roughly ground golden flaxseed
- 1 tablespoon gluten-free baking powder
- 1 teaspoon sea salt
- ½ cup vegan mayonaise
- ½ cup water
- 1 cup avocado oil, extra-virgin olive oil, or melted coconut oil
- 2 teaspoons ground cinnamon
- 1 teaspoon nutmeg
- 1 teaspoon raw wild honey

Instructions

1. Heat your waffle maker.
2. Combine flax seed with baking powder and sea salt in a large bowl and combine fully.
3. Add Mayo, water and oil to blender and blend on high for 30 seconds, until foamy
4. Mix with dry ingredients. Stir until it is all blended. The mixture should look very fluffy.
5. Let sit for 3 minutes.
6. Stir in the ground cinnamon, nutmeg, and honey.
7. Divide mixture into servings and scoop into waffler maker. Cook till it beeps.
8. Serve with extra honey if you desire syrup. Can add a few berries to the top as well.

Polenta Frittata

Ingredients

- 4-5 garlic cloves
- 1 onion
- 1 tablespoon coconut oil
- 10.5 ounces White Button mushrooms
- 1 teaspoon more coconut oil
- 1/3 cup nutritional yeast
- A pinch paprika
- A pinch cayenne (optional)
- Lots of sea salt and pepper
- Approximately 1 cup instant polenta
- 3 cups, plus 2 3/4 tablespoons vegetable broth
- 5.5 ounces cherry tomatoes, halved
- Fresh basil, for topping
- Sesame seeds, for topping

Instructions

1. Preheat oven to broil. Chop your garlic and onion, and put in a skillet with 1 tablespoon coconut oil. Cook on medium-high heat, stirring, till onion is translucent. Now chop mushrooms and add to skillet. Cook until softened (approximately 10 more minutes). Remove skillet from heat.
2. In a mixing bowl, mix polenta, nutritional yeast, paprika, cayenne, and salt and pepper. Mix to combine. Add 1 tablespoon coconut oil to pan and toss in your polenta mixture. Gradually pour in vegetable stock, beating polenta as you go to prevent lumps. Keep beating until mixture starts to bubble. Then throw in cooked veggies. Season with more sea salt and pepper.
3. Remove pan from heat. Cover polenta with chopped cherry tomatoes.
4. Place polenta frittata in the oven to broil for approximately 10 minutes, or until cherry tomatoes are bright.
5. Remove polenta frittata from oven, allow to cool slightly, and top with fresh basil leaves and sesame seeds if desired.

Hempheart Oatmeal

Ingredients

- 1 cup almond milk
- ½ cup Hemp Hearts
- 2 tablespoons freshly ground flax seed
- 1 tablespoon chia seeds
- 1 tablespoon raw wild honey
- ¾ teaspoon pure vanilla extract
- ½ teaspoon ground cinnamon

- ¼ cup crushed almonds or almond flour

Toppings

- 3 Brazil nuts
- 1 tablespoon hemphearts

Instructions

1. Add all ingredients except ground almonds and toppings to a small saucepan. Stir until combined over medium heat until it begins to boil lightly.
2. Once bubbling lightly, stir once and then leave for another 1-2 minutes.
3. Remove from the heat, stir in crushed almonds, and place in bowl. Add toppings.
4. Serve while fresh. You can garnish with a few blueberries.

Tofu Benedict

Ingredients

- 1 keto-friendly English muffin
- 2 thick slices of tomato
- 4 oz firm or extra firm tofu
- a small handful of romaine lettuce
- 1/2 small avocado
- hollandaise sauce, vegan recipe included
- salt and pepper
- 2 tablespoon coconut oil

Vegan Hollandaise Sauce

- 2 tablespoon vegan butter
- 1 tablespoon hempheart or flaxseed, ground finely
- 1/2 cup unsweetened non-dairy milk
- 1 tablespoon + 1 teaspoon nutritional yeast
- 2-3 teaspoons lemon juice, to taste
- salt and pepper
- pinch of cayenne
- pinch of turmeric, optional, for color

Instructions

For Hollandaise Sauce

1. Boil vegan butter in a small sauce pan, then whisk in flax or hemphearts until it forms a paste. Then add a bit of almond milk and stir slowly. Bring to a boil and keep whisking for 1-2 minutes. Remove from heat and add nutritional yeast, lemon juice, and seasoning. Stir well. Set aside.

To make tofu

1. Heat oil over medium heat. Slice tofu 1/2 inch thick and add salt and pepper. Place tofu in pan with hot oil and pan fry on each side for about 4-5 minutes, or until browned. Remove from heat.

To assemble the Benedict

1. Slice the English muffin in half and toast both sides with vegan butter. Then put lettuce and tomato on each slice of muffin. Then layer on tofu over the tomato and pour on Hallondaise. Add the avocado. Serve hot.

Scrambled Tofu

12 Ingredients

- 1 teaspoon nutritional yeast
- 1/4 teaspoon turmeric
- 1/4 teaspoon ground cumin
- 1/4 teaspoon paprika
- 1 tablespoon water
- Pinch sea salt
- 1/8 teaspoon black pepper
- Olive oil spray
- 1 scallion, finely diced
- 1 clove garlic, minced
- 1/2 package firm tofu, very well drained
- 1 tablespoon very finely chopped parsley

Directions

1. Mix together nutritional yeast, turmeric, cumin, paprika, water, salt, and pepper.
2. Mist a frying pan with olive oil and put over medium heat. Once heated and the oil is bubbling, add scallion and garlic. Sauté until fragrant, about 2 minutes.
3. Crumble tofu into the pan. Pour the seasoning over tofu and mix well. Cook for 2 minutes or until tofu is hot throughout.
4. Toss in parsley. Stir for another 1 to 2 minutes.
5. Serve hot with sliced avocado, vegan cheese, sliced tomato, vegan bacon, salsa, and/or hot sauce.

Lunch or Dinner Entrees

Eggplant Bird's Eye

Ingredients

- 1 whole Eggplant
- 1 Tbsp Extra Virgin Olive Oil
- 1 tsp Salted Butter
- 1 tsp Black Pepper
- 1 tsp Salt

Instructions

1. Preheat grill to high heat.
2. Rinse the eggplant, then cut into 1-inch-thick slices from end to end.
3. Brush eggplant slices with olive oil, sprinkle with salt.
4. Grill eggplant for approximately 3–4 minutes per side.
5. Cut a hole into the center of each eggplant with a cookie cutter.
6. Sauté eggplant in frying pan over medium heat with vegan butter.
7. Fill the hole with vegan cheese or tofu, your choice. You can also use soy egg mixture.
8. Cook for an additional 2–3 minutes.
9. Add salt and pepper to taste, and garnish with avocado slices or green onion.

Portobello Burgers

Marinated & grilled mushrooms:

- 2 medium large flat mushrooms such as Portobello (150 g / 5.3 oz)
- 1 tbsp coconut oil
- 1-2 tbsp freshly chopped basil
- 1 tbsp freshly chopped oregano *or* 1/2 tsp dried
- 1 clove garlic, crushed
- 1/4 tsp sea salt or more to taste
- freshly ground black pepper

Serve with:

- 2 psyllium seed buns
- 2 tbsp mayonnaise
- 2 slices vegan cheese
- 1 cup mixed lettuce

Instructions

1. Toast the buns. Marinate the mushrooms and season them with salt and pepper, crushed garlic, herbs, and coconut oil. Marinate for an hour at least.
2. Put the mushrooms top side up on a pan with melted oil. Cook over medium heat for 5 minutes. Flip and cook another five minutes.
3. Remove from heat. Top each mushroom with cheese. Then broil a few minutes to melt the cheese. That is, if you want cheese; you can make without cheese as well.
4. Start assembling the burgers by adding a tablespoon of mayo on each of the keto bun halves. Top with portobello mushrooms and lettuce and tomatoes.

Vegan Sloppy Joes

Ingredients

- 1 tbsp extra virgin olive oil
- 1/8 tsp cayenne powder
- 2 cloves of garlic
- 1 1/2 cup tomato sauce
- 2 tbsp tamari or soy sauce
- 1/4 onion
- 1/2 red bell pepper
- 1/2 green bell pepper
- 15 oz. cooked lentils
- 2 tbsp tomato paste
- 1 tbsp coconut oil
- 2 tsp garlic powder
- 2 tsp onion powder
- 1 tsp sweet paprika
- 1/8 tsp ground black pepper
- 6 slices of psyllium bread (for the buns)

Instructions

1. Heat up the olive oil and add the veggies and cayenne. Then heat over medium-high until golden brown.
2. Add the rest of the ingredients, stir, and cook for 10 minutes.
3. Heat the buns on a pan with coconut oil.
4. Spoon filling over the buns and add some shaved carrots, chili peppers, and red cabbage. Avocado is also nice on this.

Jicama Sticks

Ingredients

- 1 large Jicama peeled and cut into fries
- 1-2 tablespoons chili powder
- 1 tsp. sea salt
- Juice of 1 lime

Instructions

1. Place jicama fries in a lidded bowl. Squeeze the lime and then toss the juice to evenly cover the fries.
2. Sprinkle on chili powder and sea salt. Then put on lid and shake the container to coat.
3. Refrigerate or serve immediately.
4. Serve with a nice spicy dip or vegan guacamole.

Stuffed Mushrooms with Spinach, Vegan Cheese, and Pine Nuts

Ingredients

- 6 large cap mushrooms
- 2 cups grated vegan cheese
- ½ cup pine nuts
- 2 cups raw spinach

Instructions

1. Baste mushroom caps with coconut oil. Then stuff with spinach and cheese. You can add other ingredients like peppers if so desired.
2. Preheat oven to 400.
3. Bake 25 minutes or until cheese is golden.

Stuffed Avocados with Vegan Cheese and Black Beans

Ingredients

- 2 large avocados
- 1 cup vegan cheese
- 6 cherry tomatoes, halved
- 1 cup black beans, cooked
- 1 clove garlic, crushed
- 1 tsp black pepper
- 1 tsp cayenne
- 1 tsp paprika

Instructions

1. Cut avocados in half and hollow out pit. Then drizzle with olive oil and stuff pit with ingredients.
2. Lay the avocados on a baking sheet drizzled with oil. Lave the skins on.
3. Bake at 400 for 15 minutes.

Spicy Lentil Soup

Ingredients

- ¼ cup extra virgin olive oil
- 1 medium yellow or white onion, chopped
- 2 carrots, peeled and chopped
- 4 garlic cloves, pressed or minced
- 2 teaspoons ground cumin
- 1 teaspoon curry powder
- ½ teaspoon dried thyme
- 28 oz diced tomatoes, drained
- 1 cup brown or green lentils, rinsed and soaked overnight
- 4 cups vegetable broth
- 2 cups water
- 1 teaspoon sea salt
- 1 pinch red pepper flakes
- 1 pinch Freshly ground black pepper
- 1 cup chopped fresh collard greens or kale
- Juice of 1 medium lemon, to taste

Instructions

1. Warm the olive oil in a large pot over medium heat. Once the oil is shimmering, add the chopped onion and carrot and stir until the onion is translucent, about 5 minutes. Then add the garlic, cumin, curry powder, and thyme. Cook until fragrant while stirring constantly, for about 30 seconds. Pour in the drained diced tomatoes and cook for a few more minutes, stirring often.
2. Pour in the lentils, broth, and water. Add 1 teaspoon salt and a pinch of red pepper flakes and black pepper. Raise heat and bring to a boil, then partially cover the pot and reduce heat to simmer. Cook for 30 minutes, or until the lentils are tender but still hold their shape.
3. Pour 2 cups of the soup to a blender and blend. Pour the puréed soup back into the pot and add the chopped greens. Cook for 5 more minutes, or until the greens have softened.
4. Remove the pot from heat and stir in the lemon juice. Taste and season. Serve immediately or chill for later.

Tofu or Soy Egg Salad on a Bed of Lettuce

Ingredients:

- 15 oz tofu or soy eggs
- 1 ripe avocado, pitted
- 2 teaspoons Dijon mustard
- 1 tablespoon lemon juice
- 1/2 teaspoon sea salt
- 1/4 cup diced red onion
- 1/4 cup diced red pepper
- 1/2 cup diced cucumber
- 2 tablespoons fresh minced dill

Instructions

- In a large bowl, combine the avocado and eggs, and roughly mash with a fork to combine. Then mash in the Dijon mustard, lemon juice, salt, red onion, red pepper, cucumber, and dill and stir well to combine.
- Spoon onto a bed of lettuce.

Black Bean Burgers

Ingredients

- 16 oz black beans
- ½ green bell pepper finely chopped
- ½ onion cut up finely
- 3 cloves garlic, peeled
- 1 tbsp chili powder
- 1 tbsp cumin
- 1.2 cup bread crumbs

Instructions

1. Preheat oven to 375 degrees F (190 degrees C), and lightly oil a baking sheet.
2. In a medium bowl, mash black beans with a fork until they are thick and pasty.
3. Then finely chop bell pepper, onion, and garlic. Blend. Then stir into mashed beans.
4. Stir together soybean eggs chili powder, cumin, and chili sauce. Add into beans. Mix until thick and sticky. You can add bread crumbs now.
5. Divide into four patties and bake until crispy on foil, eight minutes per side.
6. Serve on lettuce leaves for patties with tomato, avocado, and spinach.

Zucchini Lasagna

Ingredients

Vegan Ricotta

- 3 cups (402 g) raw macadamia nuts, soaked blanched almonds*, or 1 16-ounce block extra firm tofu*, drained and pressed dry for 10 minutes)
- 2 Tbsp (6 g) nutritional yeast
- 1/2 cup (30 g) fresh basil, finely chopped
- 2 tsp dried oregano
- 1 lemon, juiced (2 Tbsp or 30 ml)
- *optional:* 1 Tbsp extra virgin olive oil (for flavor + richness)
- 1 tsp sea salt + pinch black pepper
- 1/2 cup (120 ml) water, plus more as needed (reduce if using tofu as it requires less)
- *optional:* 1/4 cup vegan parmesan cheese, plus more for topping

Pasta

- 1 28-ounce jar of organic vegan marinara sauce
- 3 zucchini squash, thinly slice

Instructions

1. Preheat oven to 375 degrees F.
2. Finely blend macadamia nuts.
3. Add nutritional yeast, fresh basil, oregano, lemon juice, olive oil (optional), salt, pepper, water, and vegan parmesan cheese (optional). Finely puree. Season as you like.
4. Pour about 1 cup marinara sauce into a small baking dish then put down a layer of zucchini.
5. Spoon ricotta over top of zucchini, spread to make a layer. Top with more zucchini and so on until you have used all the zucchini and sauce. Add vegan parmesan, cover in foil, and bake.
6. Bake covered for 45 minutes, then remove foil and bake for 15 minutes more or until you can easily spear zucchini with a fork. Let cool for 10-15 minutes before serving.
7. Serve immediately with additional vegan parmesan cheese and fresh basil. Freeze leftovers for up to a month.

Kelp Noodles with Avocado Pesto Sauce
Ingredients

- 1 package kelp noodles
- 1 half avocado
- 1 cup coconut oil or olive oil
- 1 cup kale
- ¼ cup fresh basil
- 1 tsp salt
- 1 garlic clove

Instructions

1. Soak kelp noodles for thirty minutes until they don't clump.
2. Blend all ingredients besides noodles until smooth.
3. Mix a quarter cup of pesto per cup of noodles. Then serve with your favorite oil (maybe some olive oil) on top and some oregano.

Creamy Roasted Red Pepper Soup

Ingredients

- 2 tablespoons organic coconut oil
- 2 red pepper finely chopped
- 1 large shallot, finely chopped
- 1 teaspoon celery salt
- 1 tablespoon seasoned salt
- 1 teaspoon organic paprika
- 1 pinch crushed red pepper flakes
- 4 to 5 cups of Cauliflower florets
- 4 cups vegetable stock
- 1 splash organic raw apple cider vinegar
- 1 pinch fresh thyme
- 1 cup organic coconut milk (canned)

Instructions

1. In a Dutch oven or heavy bottomed pot, heat coconut oil over medium heat.
2. Sauté chopped shallots until soft and translucent, about 3 minutes. Add chopped roasted red peppers and seasonings. Stir well to combine, allow to cook 2-3 minutes.
3. Add cauliflower, stock, vinegar, and fresh thyme. Bring to a simmer, cover pot and allow to cook for 10-15 minutes or until the cauliflower is very soft and falling apart.
4. Carefully working in small batches, puree soup until smooth in your blender*. Return fully blended soup back onto the stove and gently mix in the coconut milk.

Cream of Mushroom Soup

Ingredients

- 2 cups cauliflower florets
- 1⅔ cup unsweetened original almond milk
- 1 teaspoon onion powder
- ¼ teaspoon Himalayan rock salt
- Freshly ground pepper, to taste
- ½ teaspoon extra-virgin olive oil
- 1½ cups diced white mushrooms
- ½ yellow onion, diced

Instructions

1. Place cauliflower, milk, onion powder, salt, and pepper in a small saucepan. Cover and boil over medium heat. Reduce heat to low and simmer for an additional 7-8 minutes, until cauliflower is softened. Then, puree using a food processor, immersion blender, or blender.
2. Place oil, mushrooms, and onion in a medium-sized saucepan. Heat over high heat until onions are translucent and brown at edge, about 8 minutes.
3. Add pureed cauliflower mixture to sautéed mushrooms. Bring to a boil, cover, and simmer for 10 minutes, until thickened.
4. Serve immediately.

Harissa Portobello Tacos
Ingredients

Portobello Mushrooms

- 1 pound of portobello mushrooms
- 1/4 cup spicy harissa, or use a mild harissa
- 3 tablespoons olive oil, divided
- 1 teaspoon ground cumin
- 1 teaspoon onion powder
- 6 collard green leaves

Guacamole

- 2 medium ripe avocados
- 2 tablespoons chopped tomatoes
- 2 tablespoons chopped red onion
- 1 1/2 to 2 tablespoons lemon or lime juice
- pinch of salt
- 1 tablespoon chopped cilantro

Optional Toppings

- cashew cream
- chopped tomatoes
- chopped cilantro

Instructions

1. Remove the stem of the portobellos. Rinse mushrooms and pat dry.
2. Mix harissa, 1 1/2 tablespoons olive oil, cumin, and onion powder in a bowl. Brush each mushroom with the harissa mixture, making sure to cover the edges of the mushroom as well. Let mushroom marinade for 15 minutes.
3. While the mushrooms are marinating, prepare guacamole. Halve and pit the avocados and scoop out the flesh. Mash avocados and mix in chopped tomatoes, red onion, lemon (or lime) juice, salt, and cilantro. Set aside.
4. Rinse collard greens. Chop off the tough stems and set aside.
5. When the mushrooms are done marinating, heat 1 1/2 tablespoons of olive oil in a skillet or sauté pan over medium-high heat. Place the portobello mushrooms in the pan and cook for 3 minutes. Flip over and cook for another 2 to 3 minutes. Each side should be browned.
6. Turn off the heat and let the mushrooms rest for 2 to 3 minutes before slicing.
7. Take a collard green leaf and fill it with a few slices of portobello. Add guacamole, chopped tomatoes, cashew cream, and cilantro to your liking.

7 Sauces, Dressings, and Dips

Spinach Artichoke Dip

Ingredients

- 1/4 cup vegan parmesan
- 1 tbsp. olive oil
- 3 large cloves garlic diced
- 12 oz. marinated artichoke hearts* chopped into bite sized pieces
- 4 cups baby spinach diced
- 1/4 cup vegan mayo
- 8 oz. vegan cream cheese
- 1/2 tsp. garlic powder
- salt and pepper to taste

Instructions

1. Preheat oven to 400 degrees.
2. Heat olive oil in a pan over medium heat. Add garlic and sauté for a minute, stirring frequently. Put in artichoke hearts and spinach and sauté until the spinach is wilted. Add vegan cream cheese, mayo, garlic powder, salt, and pepper and stir to combine.
3. Put in a baking dish and top with parmesan and bake in the oven for 5 minutes. Turn oven to broil and cook for an additional 3-5 minutes.

Jalapeno Hummus

Ingredients

- 2 cans chickpeas
- 1/3 cup tahini paste
- 8 roasted garlic cloves
- 2-5 jalapeños seeded
- 1/3 cup cilantro chopped
- 1/4 cup fresh lemon juice or more to taste
- 1 tbsp extra virgin olive oil
- 1 1/2 tsp cumin
- 3/4 tsp salt or more to taste

Instructions

1. Drain chickpeas and pop to remove skins.
2. Put chickpeas, tahini paste, roasted garlic, seeded jalapeños, chopped cilantro, lemon juice, olive oil, cumin, and salt into a food processor.
3. Blend until smooth. Taste and add more jalapenos if you desire more heat.
4. Serve with veggies.

Spicy Peanut Sauce

Ingredients

- 1/2 cup salted natural peanut or almond butter
- 1 1/2 Tbsp tamair sauce
- 2-3 Tbsp brown honey
- 1/2 lime, juiced
- 1/2 tsp chili garlic sauce
- 1/2 tsp fresh grated ginger (optional)
- hot water to thin

Instructions

1. Add all ingredients but water to a bowl. Whisk together well.
2. Then add boiling water 1 tsp at a time till it thickens.
3. Serve with veggie rolls, Jicama sticks, or as a dipping sauce for cucumbers and bell peppers.

Vegan Ranch Dressing

Ingredients

- 1 cup vegan mayonnaise
- 1/4 cup soy milk
- 1 tsp garlic powder
- 1 tsp onion powder
- 1/4 tsp salt
- dash fresh ground black pepper, or to taste
- 1 tbsp apple cider vinegar (regular vinegar is also ok, but apple cider is better)
- 2 tsp fresh chopped parsley
- 1/2 tsp fresh chopped dill

Instructions

1. Place all of the ingredients except for the parsley and the dill in a blender or food processor and process until smooth and creamy.
2. Mix in the fresh chopped parsley and dill, then pulse together just until the parsley and dill are both very finely minced.
3. Season to taste.
4. Transfer to a small bowl or serving container and allow to thicken as it cools.

Vegan Italian Dressing

Ingredients

- 1/2 cup extra-virgin olive oil
- 2 tablespoons apple cider vinegar
- 1 tablespoon fresh lemon juice
- 1 tablespoon finely chopped flat-leaf parsley
- 1 tablespoon Italian seasoning
- 1 teaspoon minced garlic
- 1/2 teaspoon onion powder
- 1/2 teaspoon pure maple syrup
- 1/4 teaspoon Celtic sea salt, plus more to taste
- 1/4 teaspoon freshly ground black pepper, plus more to taste

Instructions

1. Mix all ingredients in a jar, secure the lid, and shake vigorously until totally combined.
2. Chill in the fridge. Will keep for about 5 days.

Creamy Avocado Sauce

Ingredients

- 1 ripe avocado
- 1 small garlic clove, peeled
- 2 tsps fresh-squeezed lemon juice
- 1 tsp olive oil
- ¼ cup fresh basil leaves
- Sea salt and pepper

Instructions

1. Add basil and garlic to a blender and blend finely.
2. Then add avocado, olive oil, and lemon juice and blend until smooth.
3. Seaon with sea salt and pepper.
4. You can put this on salads, Jacimi sticks, cucumber slices, avocados, or zucchini noodles.

Almond Feta

Ingredients

- 1 cup almonds, soaked for at least 8 hours
- 3 tablespoons lemon juice or white wine vinegar
- 3 tablespoons olive oil
- 1 garlic clove
- 1/2 teaspoon salt
- 4-8 tablespoons water

Instructions

1. Soak almonds overnight. Squeeze to pop them out of skins. Then blend with lemon juice, oil, garlic and salt. Add extra water as needed.
2. Put a colander in a bowl and cover with cheesecloth. Squeeze the pureed mixture into cheese, then cover and let set for 24 hours at room temperature.
3. Preheat oven to 400 F and cover a baking sheet with parchment paper. Place cheese on paper and smooth out into a wheel shape.
4. Bake for 30 minutes or until firm.
5. Serve fresh or chilled. It will last for a week if refrigerated.

7 Vegan Fat Bombs

Nutty Coconut Balls

Ingredients

- 1 1/2 cups walnuts or nut of choice
- 1/2 cup shredded coconut
- 1/4 cup coconut butter + 1 tablespoon extra if needed
- 2 tablespoons almond butter or nut butter of choice
- 2 tablespoons chia seeds
- 2 tablespoons flax meal
- 2 tablespoons hemp seeds
- 1 teaspoon cinnamon
- 1/2 teaspoon vanilla bean powder
- 1/4 teaspoon kosher salt
- 2 tablespoons cacao nibs

For the chocolate drizzle

- 1 oz. bittersweet or unsweetened chocolate chopped
- 1/2 teaspoon coconut oil

Instructions

1. In the food processor bowl or blender, combine all of the ingredients except for the cacao nibs. Pulse for about 1-2 minutes or until the mixture starts to break down. It should be crumbly. Keep going until oils let the mixture stick together well. If your mixture seems dry, you may need the extra tablespoon of coconut butter to help it come together. Once the mixture is sticking together well, pulse in the cacao nibs, just to incorporate them.
2. Use a tablespoon scoop to divide the mixture into even amounts. Then mold into balls with your hands. Set on a plate.
3. Melt the chocolate and coconut oil together in the microwave for 1 minute, or until it's completely melted. Drizzle over balls and place in the fridge to harden. Sprinkle coconut flakes or shreds on top to taste. Or use orange zest if you prefer.
4. Store in an airtight container.

No Bake Oatmeal Fudge Bars

Ingredients

Crust and Topping

- 1 cup coconut oil
- ¼ cup xylitol
- 2 cups hemp hearts
- ½ cup shredded coconut, unsweetened
- ⅓ cup coconut flour
- ½ teaspoon vanilla extract

Fudge

- 10 oz. (285 grams) unsweetened chocolate
- ½ cup (118 mL) full-fat coconut milk
- 10 drops alcohol-free stevia

Instructions

1. Line a baking sheet with parchment paper and fold over sides so that you can lift it easily.
2. Melt coconut oil and xylitol in a large saucepan over medium heat. Whisk until xylitol granules have dissolved, about 2 minutes.
3. Mix in the Hemp Hearts, shredded coconut, coconut flour, and vanilla extract. Take off the heat and combine with a spoon until the ingredients are well blended. Press half of mixture into the bottom of the prepared pan. Set aside rest for a topping.
4. Place the base in the refrigerator.
5. Melt chocolate and coconut milk in a small heavy saucepan over low heat, stirring until smooth. Add stevia and set aside.
6. Take the chocolate out of the fridge and spoon over the crust in the pan and spread around.
7. Crumble hemp over the chocolate and then cover and refrigerate for at least 3 hours. Cut into bars.

Chocolate Almond Butter Cups

Ingredients

- 1 cup chocolate paste
- 2 cups coconut oil
- 1 cup almond butter
- 1 tsp almond extract
- 2 tbsp ground cinnamon

Instructions

1. Fill a pan with muffin cups. Melt some chocolate past with coconut oil, add a hint of cinnamon and almond extract, and pour into cups. Then set in fridge to harden.
2. Melt coconut butter, almond butter, and ground cinnamon. Pour over set chocolate cups. Let set ten minutes.
3. Mix a half cup of creamy coconut butter with a half cup of melted coconut oil and stir. Pour over cups.
4. Garnish each cup with an almond.

Lemon Fat Bombs

Ingredients

- 7.1 oz coconut butter, softened
- $1/4$ cup extra virgin coconut oil, softened
- 1-2 tbsp organic lemon zest *or* 1-2 tsp lemon juice
- 15-20 drops Stevia extract (Clear or Lemon)
- 1 pinch sea salt or pink Himalayan salt

Instructions

1. Zest the lemons and make sure the coconut butter and coconut oil are softened (room temperature). It's better if you use a very fine grater to avoid having large pieces of lemon peel in the fat bombs. *Make sure you use organic, unwaxed lemons in this recipe.*
2. Mix all the ingredients in a bowl and make sure the lemon zest and stevia are distributed evenly. You can use clear, lemon or coconut stevia drops.
3. Fill each mini muffin paper cup, or silicone candy mold with ~ 1 tbsp of the coconut mixture and place on a tray that will fit in the fridge.
4. Place in the fridge for 30-60 minutes or until solid. Keep refrigerated.

Pumpkin Pie Bites
Ingredients

- 1/2 cup pumpkin puree
- 2 oz. coconut butter
- 1/2 cup coconut oil
- 2 tsp cinnamon
- 1/2 cup pecans

Instructions

1. Melt down your coconut oil and butter until soft.
2. Combine the pumpkin puree, coconut butter, and coconut oil in a mixing bowl and stir until completely combined.
3. Add honey and cinnamon.
4. Once your fat bomb batter is combined, pour into an ice cube tray and let set.
5. Toast chopped pecans on a dry pan on medium heat until slightly browned and fragrant.
6. Top each fat bomb with some pecan pieces.
7. Refrigerate until set.

Green Truffles

Ingredients

- 1 ½ cups unsweetened medium-shredded coconut
- 2 tablespoons Spirulina powder
- 1 tbsp vanilla extract
- ½ cup [extra-virgin coconut oil](), melted

Optional toppings

- Hemp hearts
- Chia seeds
- Unsweetened medium-shredded coconut

Instructions

1. Line a small baking sheet with parchment paper and set aside.
2. Add coconut and Spirulina to a blender or food processor. Mix until coconut is covered in greens, then add in coconut oil.
3. Mix until everything is combined. Should be sticky.
4. Scoop one tablespoon of dough and roll into ball. Place on transfer sheet.
5. Cool for 15 minutes in the fridge.
6. Store in the fridge for 5 days, or freezer for 2 months.

7 Salads

Palm Hearts Salad

Ingredients

- 1 can hearts of palm
- 1 avocado
- 3 green onions, chopped and white parts discarded
- Juice of 1 lime
- 1/2 cup finely chopped cilantro

Instructions

1. Chop avocado and toss with cilantro and lime juice. Then blend to a fine puree.
2. Chop up palm hearts. Then add puree and stir until coated.
3. Season with salt. Add green onions as garnish.

Rich Vegetable Salad

Ingredients

- 1 handful of romaine, finely chopped
- 1 handful iceberg, finely chopped
- 1 cup Brussel sprouts, chopped
- 1 cup finely chopped asparagus
- 1 cup chopped celery
- 1 cup colorful sweet peppers
- 1 avocado, peeled and chopped
- 1 handful spring greens
- 1 handful red cabbage
- 1 handful dandelion greens
- ½ cucumber chopped
- 4 baby carrots, chopped
- Alfalfa sprouts if desired

Instructions

1. Steam Brussel sprouts.
2. Combine all ingredients. Garnish as desired and top with vegan ranch or another dressing.

Cajun Tempeh Chicken Salad

Ingredients

- 12 ounces tempeh, cubed
- 1 stalk celery, minced
- 1 large dill pickle, minced
- 2 -3 scallions, minced
- 2 tablespoons red bell peppers, minced
- 1 tablespoon fresh parsley, chopped
- ½ cup soy mayonnaise
- 1 tablespoon yellow mustard
- 1 teaspoon lemon juice
- Salt and black pepper

Instructions

1. Poach tempeh in coconut oil. Chop finely and set in fridge.
2. Combine celery, pepper, pickle, scallions, and parsley.
3. Add tempeh, vegan mayonnaise, mustard, lemon juice, salt, and pepper to vegetables.

Leafy Green Salad

Ingredients

- Handful romaine lettuce
- Handful spinach
- Handful kale
- Handful spring greens
- 1 tomato
- 1 green onion, finely chopped

Instructions

1. Toss all ingredients together.
2. Toss with oil and apple cider vinegar.

Southwestern Tofu Salad with Black Beans and Lime Dressing

Ingredients

For The Tofu

- 14-16 ounces block extra firm tofu, drained
- 1 1/2 tablespoons Tamari
- 1 teaspoon ground cumin
- 1 teaspoon onion powder
- 1/2 teaspoon paprika
- 1/2 teaspoon garlic powder
- 1/2 teaspoon dried oregano
- Pinch Cayenne pepper
- 1-2 tablespoons olive oil

For The Salad

- 4 cups Romaine lettuce, chopped
- 14 ounce can black beans, drained and rinsed
- 1 ripe avocado, chopped
- 1 cup cherry or grape tomatoes, cut in halves
- 1/2 cup sweet corn kernels
- 1/2 cup red bell pepper, chopped
- 1/4 cup red onion, chopped
- 1/4 cup cilantro leaves, chopped

Lime Dressing

- 1 medium lime, juiced
- 2 tablespoons olive oil
- 1 teaspoon maple syrup
- 1/2 teaspoon ground cumin
- 1 teaspoon green onion, chopped
- 1 clove garlic, minced
- 1/2 teaspoon salt

Instructions

1. Place tofu cubes in a bowl and toss with Bragg's liquid aminos, cumin, paprika, garlic powder, onion powder, dried oregano, and cayenne pepper. Marinate for at least 10 minutes.
2. Heat oil in a large non-stick skillet over medium heat. Cook the tofu cubes until brown and crispy on all sides. Turn off heat.
3. For the dressing, mix lime juice, olive oil, maple syrup, cumin, green onions, garlic and salt in a jar. Shake well.
4. Put chopped lettuce on the base of the plate, then put on black beans, avocado, cherry tomatoes, bell pepper, onion, and cilantro. Drizzle with lime dressing.

Vegan Chef's Salad

Ingredients

- 6 cups (torn iceberg lettuce
- 2 cups torn radicchio lettuce
- 1/2 cup alfalfa sprouts
- 4 radishes, thinly sliced
- 3/4 cup sliced cucumber
- 1/3 cup thinly sliced sweet onion
- 1/2 cup rinsed drained canned chickpeas
- 3 tofu chunks
- 1 large tomato, cut into 12 wedges
- 1/2 avocado, pitted, peeled, and sliced
- 2 oz vegan Swiss cheese, julienned
- 2 oz vegan Cheddar cheese

Instructions

1. Toss fresh ingredients and tofu together.
2. Spoon oil and vinegar or other dressing over top. Add cheese to top.

Vegan Cobb Salad

Ingredients

- Romaine Lettuce (2 to 3 heads cut Romaine)
- 4 grilled asparagus spears, cut
- 3/4 cup green beans, cut
- 1/2 cup cubed roasted golden beets (can buy at Whole Foods or somewhere similar)
- 1/2 avocado, cubed
- 1 cup cucumber, peeled and cubed
- cherry tomatoes, cut in half
- 3/4 cup garbanzo beans, rinsed and soaked overnight
- 3 tablespoons slivered almonds
- sunflower seeds to sprinkle on top
- cracked pepper – optional

Instructions

1. Layer greens and beans.
2. Sprinkle sunflower seeds, almonds, and pepper on top.

7 Smoothies

Iced Coffee

Ingredients

- 1 ¾ cup brewed coffee or tea
- 1 tablespoon almond butter
- 2 tbsp hemp hearts
- 10 grams cacao butter (about 4-5 wafers)
- 1 tablespoon coconut oil
- ¼ teaspoon ground vanilla bean, optional
- ¼ teaspoon ground cinnamon, optional
- 4-6 ice cubes

Toppings

- ¼ cup coconut whipped cream
- 1 teaspoon cacao nibs

Instructions

1. Blend coffee, almond butter, cacao butter, vanilla, and cinnamon in a blender. Pour into a jar and place in the fridge to cool completely.
2. Once chilled, place back in your blender. Add 4-6 ice cubes.
3. Blend until smooth.
4. Pour into a jar, top with coconut whipped cream and cacao nibs, and enjoy!

Cinnamon Chocolate Breakfast Smoothie

Ingredients

- 3/4 cup coconut milk
- 1/2 ripe avocado
- 2 teaspoons unsweetened cacao powder
- 1 teaspoon cinnamon powder
- 1/4 teaspoon vanilla extract
- Stevia to taste
- 1 teaspoon coconut oil (optional)

Instructions

1. Blend all the ingredients together well.
2. Serve chilled.

Green Coffee Shake

Ingredients

1. 1 13.5 fl. oz. (400 ml) can of full-fat coconut milk
2. 1½ cup cold brewed coffee (decaf or regular) black
3. 2 tablespoons unsweetened almond butter
4. 1 tablespoon vanilla extract
5. 8 ice cubes

Instructions

1. Place all ingredients but ice in the jug of your blender. Blend for 10 seconds, or until smooth.
2. Divide between four 10 fl. oz. (300 ml) glasses, drop two ice cubes in each glass, and enjoy.

Coffee and Chocolate Smoothie

Ingredients

- ¾ cups cold brewed coffee
- 1 cup dark chocolate
- 1 drizzle vegan chocolate sauce
- 5 oz vegan yogurt
- 1 ½ cup ice cubes

Instructions

1. Blend all ingredients thoroughly.
2. Drizzle chocolate over the top.

Blueberry Smoothie

Ingredients

- coconut milk
- blueberries
- stevia
- vanilla extract
- virgin coconut oil (optional but recommended)
- gelatin (optional but recommended)
- 3 ice cubes

Instructions

1. Blend until smooth, adding more milk if too thick or more ice if too watery.

Chocolate Almond Smoothie

Ingredients

- almond milk
- 3 ice cubes
- stevia
- almond butter
- cacao powder
- avocado

Instructions

1. Blend all ingredients until smooth. Add more almond milk if too thick or more ice if too watery.

Lemon Ginger Green Smoothie

Ingredients

- Kale
- cilantro
- fresh ginger root
- lemon
- cucumber

Instructions

1. Blend all together thoroughly.
2. Top with cilantro and a lemon slice.

7 Desserts

Chia Pudding

- 3/4 cup (175 ml) coconut milk
- 1.5 Tablespoons chia seeds
- Raw honey to taste (optional)

Instructions

1. Place the coconut milk, chia seeds, and honey into a cup with a lid and shake well for 5-10 seconds.
2. Pour the viscous mixture into a glass and place into fridge for at least 4 hours. It will puff up, don't worry.
3. Mix the diced strawberries, blueberries, blackberries, matcha powder, cocoa powder, or other ingredients into the pudding and serve chilled. You can add whatever ingredients you want as long as it is keto-friendly.

Coconut Chocolate Cups
Coconut Candies:

- 1/2 cup coconut butter
- 1/2 cup virgin organic coconut oil
- 1/2 cup unsweetened shredded coconut
- 3 tbsp honey

Chocolate Topping:

- 1 & 1/2 ounces Cocoa Butter
- 1 ounce unsweetened chocolate
- 1/4 cup cocoa powder
- 1/4 tsp vanilla extract

Instructions

1. Line a mini-muffin pan with 20 mini paper liners.
2. Combine coconut butter and coconut oil in a small saucepan over low heat. Stir until melted and smooth, then stir in shredded coconut and honey until combined.
3. Divide mixture among prepared mini muffin cups and freeze until firm, about 30 minutes.
4. For the chocolate coating, combine cocoa butter and unsweetened chocolate together in bowl set over a pan of simmering water. Stir until melted.
5. Stir in cocoa powder, until smooth.
6. Remove from heat and add vanilla extract.
7. Spoon chocolate topping over chilled coconut candies and let set for about 15 minutes.

Poached Pears with Dark Chocolate

Ingredients

- 3 firm pears
- 3 cups organic coconut palm sugar
- Zest of one lemon
- Vanilla extract

Instructions

1. Boil water with sugar, lemon zest, and vanilla. When boiling, add peeled pears. Poach.
2. Melt the coconut butter and chocolate over low heat. Drizzle heavily over poached pears.

Blueberry Soy Cheesecake

Ingredients

For the Crust:
- 1 pack almonds, finely ground
- 1 stick vegan margarine

For the Filling
- 4 packages dairy-free cream cheese (8 ounces each)
- 1 1/4 cup sugar
- egg Replacer for 4 eggs
- 1/3 cup dairy-free sour cream (such as Tofutti Sour Supreme)
- 1 teaspoon vanilla extract
- *For the Topping*
- 4 tablespoons dairy-free sour cream (more or less as needed)
- Pureed blueberries
- Vanilla extract

Instructions

1. Melt margarine and stir in almond meal. Pack down into pie pan.
2. Mix cream cheese till smooth. Throw in sugar and egg replacer. Then add lemon juice, sour cream, lemon zest, and lemon extract.
3. Pour into crust and then bake for 1 hour at 350.
4. Fill cracks with melted cream cheese.
5. Cool for two hours. Then pour on blueberries mixed with vanilla extract.

No-Crust Apple Pie

Ingredients

- 5-6 large organic apples (about 3 lb.), sliced thin
- zest and juice of 1 small organic lemon
- 2 Tbsp coconut oil
- 1/4 tsp allspice
- 1/4 tsp nutmeg
- 1/2 tsp cinnamon
- 1/2 tsp salt
- 1/4 cup honey
- 1/4 cup tapioca flour (optional)

Instructions

1. Mix apples and lemon juice and zest.
2. Cook with coconut oil over low heat until simmering. Then add in all other ingredients. Combine well.
3. Cook for 5 minutes.
4. Put pecans, cinnamon, and honey in a bowl and mix them.
5. Scoop cooked apple filling into a cup. Add pecans and then enjoy warm.

Walnuts with Dark Chocolate

Ingredients

- 1 package walnuts
- 1 dark chocolate bar
- Juice of 1 lime if desired
- 1 cup coconut oil or butter

Instructions

1. Toast walnuts on a tray in 250 heat.
2. Melt chocolate and coconut butter over low heat until smooth. Pour over walnuts. Squeeze on lime juice if desired for extra tang.

Chocolate Silk Pie with Almond Crust

Ingredients

Crust

- 1 1/2 cups raw almonds
- 1/3 cup unsweetened cacao powder
- 1 heaping (packed) cup pitted dates, soaked for 10 minutes in warm water and then drained

Filling:

- 12 ounces silken tofu, drained, patted dry
- 1 3/4 cups dairy-free semisweet chocolate chips
- 1/2 cup light or full fat coconut milk (or other dairy-free milk)

Instructions

1. Pulse nuts and cocoa powder in a food processor until it reaches a fine meal. Remove and set aside. Then process dates until it is sticky. Add to almond meal and process until all combined.
2. Oil glass pan with coconut oil and then press down crust. Make it go up the sides.
3. Melt chocolate, stirring frequently. Blend with tofu and almond milk until it is a fine brown paste.
4. Pour over crust and smooth down with spatula. Cover and freeze or refrigerate until set.

Download KETO SMOOTHIES eBook - completely FREE!

Low carb smoothies are among the best treats on the ketogenic diet. So good and nutritious, they make meals simple and quick, and can also be effective instant cures when you're fighting the dreaded keto flu.

They're perfect anytime, but especially when you're not hungry but you need to fill up. The best keto smoothie recipes are those engineered to help you achieve your fat, protein and micronutrient macros while staying very low carb.

Go to **NJKETO.COM/SMOOTHIES** and get instant free access.

Limited time offer.

References

1. Healthline. *The Vegan Diet.* https://www.healthline.com/nutrition/vegan-diet-guide#section3.
2. Eat for Health. Daily Nutrient Requirements Calculator. https://www.eatforhealth.gov.au/page/eat-health-calculators/calculated/1467294092.
3. The Vegan Society. *Nutrition Overview.* https://www.vegansociety.com/resources/nutrition-and-health/nutrition-overview.
4. Health Hub by Sun Warrior. *45 Super Foods You Should Be Eating.* https://sunwarrior.com/healthhub/45-superfoods-to-add-to-your-diet.
5. Fetters, Aleisha. *What's Up with the High-Fat Diet Trend, and Does it Work?* Women's Health. https://www.womenshealthmag.com/weight-loss/a19982439/ketogenic-diet/.
6. WebMD. *Nutrition and Healthy Eating.* https://www.mayoclinic.org/healthy-lifestyle/nutrition-and-healthy-eating/expert-answers/mufas/faq-20057775.
7. Vegan at Heart. *Top 8 Benefits of the Vegan Ketogenic Diet.* http://www.veganatheart.org/benefits-of-vegan-keto/.
8. Dr. Axe. *Vegan Keto Diet and Vegetarian Keto Diet: Can They Be Done?* https://draxe.com/hub/keto-diet/vegetarian-vegan-keto-diet/.
9. Ketogenic Supplement Reviews. *A Simple Guide to the Keto Vegan Diet.* https://www.ketogenicsupplementreviews.com/ketosis-diet/vegan/.
10. Perfect Keto. *108 Foods to Avoid.* https://www.perfectketo.com/ketogenic-diet-foods-to-avoid/.
11. Wayne, Jake. *How Many Calories Should I Eat Working Out?* Livestrong. https://www.livestrong.com/article/437419-how-long-after-i-work-out-should-i-eat/.
12. Dr. Axe. *Overcoming Keto Flu Symptoms.* https://draxe.com/hub/keto-diet/keto-flu-symptoms/.
13. Johnson, Addision. *7-Day Vegetarian Keto Diet Plan & Menu.* EatingWell. https://dietingwell.com/vegetarian-keto-diet/.

Made in the USA
Middletown, DE
30 December 2018